CW00327006

THE INVINCIBLE IRON MAN

EXTREMIS

Reader Services

CUSTOMER SERVICE IN THE UK AND REPUBLIC OF IRELAND
How to continue your collection:
Customers can either place an order with their newsagent or receive issues on subscription.
Back issues: Either order through your newsagent or write to: Marvel Collection, Jacklin Enterprises UK, PO Box 77, Jarrow, NE32 3YH, enclosing payment of the cover price plus £1.00 p&p per copy. (Republic of Ireland: cover price plus €1.75).
Subscriptions: You can have your issues sent directly to your home. For details, see insert in issue 1 or phone our Customer Service Hotline on 0871 472 4240 (Monday to Friday, 9am-5pm, calls cost 10p per minute from UK landline). Alternatively you can write to Marvel Collection, Jacklin Enterprises UK, PO Box 77, Jarrow, NE32 3YH, or fax your enquiries to 0871 472 4241, or e-mail: marvelcollection@jacklinservice.com or visit www.graphicnovelcollection.com

CUSTOMER SERVICE IN OVERSEAS MARKETS

Australia: Back issues can be ordered from your newsagent. Alternatively telephone (03) 9872 4000 or write to: Back Issues Department, Bissett Magazine Services, PO Box 3460, Nunawading Vic 3131. Please enclose payment of the cover price, plus A$2.49 (inc. GST) per issue postage and handling. Back issues are subject to availability.
Subscriptions: You can have your issues sent directly to your home. For details, see insert in issue 1 or phone our Customer Service Hotline on (03) 9872 4000. Alternatively you can write to Hachette subs offer, Bissett Magazine Services, PO Box 3460, Nunawading Vic 3131, or fax your enquiries to (03) 9873 4988, or order online at www.bissettmags.com.au

New Zealand: For back issues, ask your local magazine retailer or write to: Netlink, PO Box 47906, Ponsonby, Auckland.
South Africa: Back issues are available through your local CNA store or other newsagent.
Subscriptions: call (011) 265 4309, fax (011) 314 2984, or write to: Marvel Collection, Private Bag 10, Centurion 0046 or e-mail: service@jacklin.co.za
Malta: Back issues are only available through your local newsagent.
Malaysia: Call (03) 8023 3260, or e-mail: sales@allscript.com
Singapore: Call (65) 287 7090, or e-mail: sales@allscript.com

Published by Hachette Partworks Ltd, Jordan House, 47 Brunswick Place, London, N1 6EB
www.hachettepartworks.co.uk

Distributed in the UK and Republic of Ireland by Marketforce

This special edition published in 2012 by Hachette Partworks Ltd. forming part of The Ultimate Marvel Graphic Novel Collection.

Printed in China
ISBN: 978-1-906965-96-9

Licensed by Marvel Characters B.V. through Panini S.p.A., Italy. All Rights Reserved.

THE INVINCIBLE IRON MAN ™

WARREN ELLIS
WRITER

ADI GRANOV
ART

TERRY AUSTIN
INKS

VIRTUAL CALLIGRAPHY'S RANDY GENTILE
LETTERS

TOM BREVOORT
EDITOR

JOE QUESADA
EDITOR IN CHIEF

THE INVINCIBLE
IRON MAN: EXTREMIS

Marco M. Lupoi
*Panini Publishing Director
(Europe)*

Capitalist businessman, genius military industrialist and socialite playboy, tormented with a self-loathing and driven by alcoholism, Tony Stark aka Iron Man is a super-hero with whom it should be hard to identify with, at least in theory. However, his adventures have spanned other worlds, other times, and most of the countries of this planet, and have managed to capture the imagination of generations of readers for almost five decades. A Marvel-style tycoon in an armoured super suit, saving the day and winning accolades along the way with two huge movie hits to underline his popularity as a comic book icon, IRON MAN is one of the leading heroes of the House of Ideas. On the outside he's invulnerable - untouchable, even. But inside, our Golden Avenger is a wounded figure with a conscience, and it is this contrasting psyche that strikes a chord with readers around the world.

And so when self-confessed technology futurist Warren Ellis was given the task of writing a modern Iron Man story, it was a perfect match, especially with Adi Granov's unique and glorious art style complementing Warren's vision. Equally rewarding to both well-read Iron Man fans and new readers, *Extremis* is THE Iron Man tale of the noughties, the one that visually inspired the first Iron Man movie, bringing the character's origins to the fore and sharing a vision of the future to come...

"It's about becoming better. It's about bringing on the future. The earliest stages of adapting machine to man and making us great."

ntains material originally published in magazine form as The Invincible Iron Man Vol. 4 #1-6. Senior Editor (Hachette Partworks Ltd.), Sarah Gale. Packaged by Panini Publishing, a division of Panini ited. Mike Riddell, Managing Director. Alan O'Keefe, Managing Editor. Simon Frith, Senior Editor. Ed Hammond, Editor. Marco M. Lupoi, Publishing Director Europe.
Warran-Smith, Designer. Additional content: Mike Conroy. Office of publication: Brockbourne House, 77 Mount Ephraim, Tunbridge Wells, Kent TN4 8BS. No similarity between any of the names, racters, persons and/or institutions in this edition with those of any living or dead person or institution is intended, and any such similarity which may exist is purely coincidental. This publication may

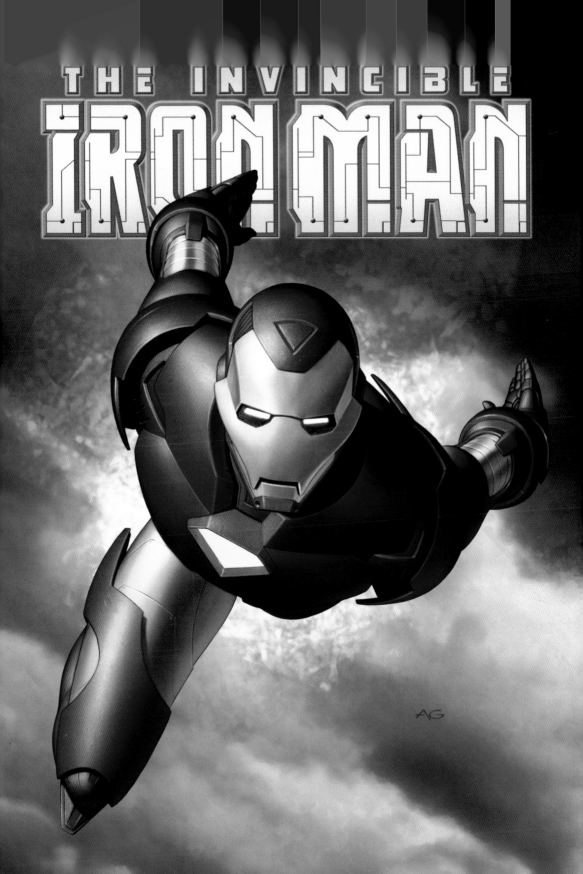

IRON MAN

EXTREMIS

ONE OF SIX

Written by Warren Ellis
Illustrated by Adi Granov

MALLEN. YOU'RE SURE YOU'RE UP FOR THIS?

JUST DO IT.

Lettering by UC's Randy Gentile
Assistant Editors: Schmidt, Wiley & Lazer
Editor: Tom Brevoort

Editor in chief: Joe Quesada
Publisher: Dan Buckley

PSST!

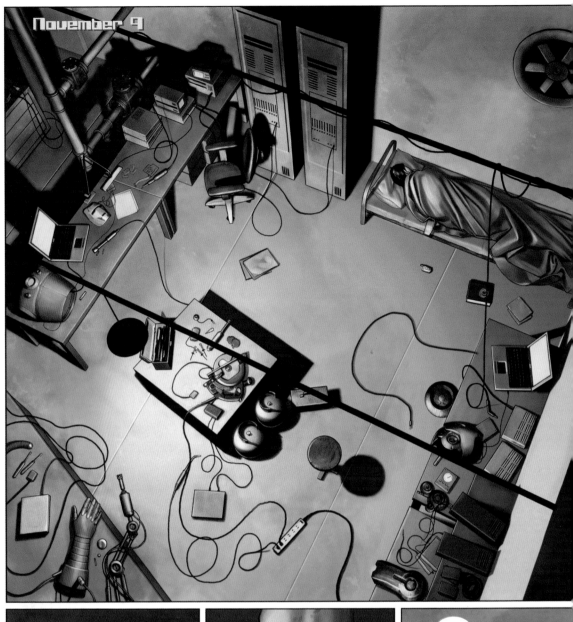

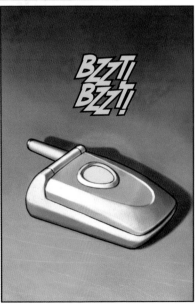

BZZT!
BZZT!

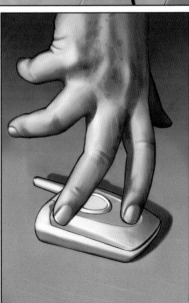

YEAH.

MR. STARK?

YEAH.

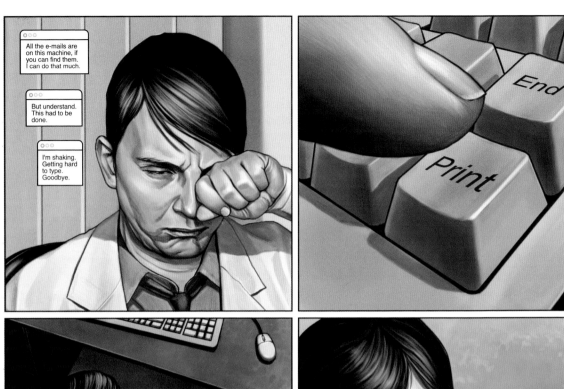

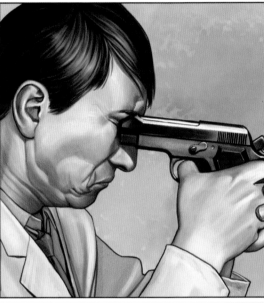

"MY DAD USED TO TELL ME CONEY ISLAND WAS THE MOST FABULOUS PLACE IN THE WORLD."

THE AMUSEMENTS. THE FANTASTIC CONSTRUCTIONS.

PEOPLE BELIEVED THEY HAD TO BE LIVING IN THE FUTURE, TO BE ABLE TO VISIT A PLACE LIKE CONEY ISLAND.

AND AT NIGHT THEY WOULDN'T GO HOME. THEY'D SLEEP ON THE BEACH, SO THEY COULD WAKE UP IN THIS FUTURE PLACE.

TONY. WOULD IT BE FAIR TO DEFINE YOU AS AN ARMS DEALER?

I DON'T THINK SO. I MEAN, I WOULDN'T DENY THAT--

BUT YOU DO DESIGN AND SELL ARMS?

I WOULDN'T DENY THAT WE HAVE DESIGNED ARMS FOR THE U.S. MILITARY, OF COURSE.

IN FACT, STARK INTERNATIONAL WAS FOUNDED ON WEAPONEERING, I BELIEVE.

MY FIRST MAJOR CONTRACT WAS FOR THE U.S. AIR FORCE, YES.

WHAT WAS THAT CONTRACT?

MY INITIAL ENGINEERING INTEREST WAS IN MINIATURIZATION. THE USAF SAW APPLICATIONS IN MUNITIONS.

AND THAT WAS THE SEEDPOD BOMB, YES?

IT WAS. THE SAME PROCESS, HOWEVER, LED TO--

THE SEEDPOD WAS FIRST USED IN GULF WAR ONE? HOW OLD WERE YOU?

I WAS MAYBE NINETEEN. I FORGET.

NOW, CORRECT ME IF I'M WRONG, BUT THE SEEDPOD DISPENSED HUNDREDS OF "SMART" MICROMUNITIONS FROM A MOTHER BOMB CASING, YES?

...YES. IT WAS INTENDED TO DESTROY AIRFIELDS AND CRIPPLE ARMORED CONVOYS.

DID THEY ALL WORK?

EXCUSE ME?

DID ALL OF THOSE BOMBLETS GO OFF AS ANTICIPATED?

YOU'D HAVE TO ASK THE MILITARY, WE NEVER GOT AN OPERATIONS REPORT ON EVERY SINGLE MICROMUNITION. THERE WERE TENS OF THOUSANDS--

PERHAPS YOU'D LIKE TO LOOK AT THESE PICTURES.

ACH ONE OF YOUR BOMBLETS HAS THE EXPLOSIVE FORCE OF THREE STICKS OF DYNAMITE.

EIGHTEEN PERCENT OF THEM SUFFERED TIMER FAILURES. THEY'RE CATTERED ACROSS THE THEATER OF CONFLICT.

CHILDREN FIND THEM, TONY.

CAN YOU TELL US WHAT THE STARK SENTINEL IS?

...IT'S A LANDMINE.

AGAIN, DESIGNED WHEN YOU WERE IN YOUR EARLY TWENTIES?

YES. MANY OF THEM RM THE DEFENSIVE LINE BETWEEN ORTH AND SOUTH KOREA.

YOU'RE UNAWARE OF STARK LANDMINES IN, SAY, EAST TIMOR?

YES.

REPORTEDLY, YOU YOURSELF WERE INJURED BY ONE OF YOUR OWN LANDMINES.

YES.

I'D BEEN ASKED TO LOOK AT WAYS TO CONTAIN AL QAEDA IN AFGHANISTAN. I WENT OUT THERE TO CONSULT.

THERE WAS A SKIRMISH WITH TALIBAN GUNMEN.

I'M FINE NOW, THANKS.

WAS THAT BEFORE OR AFTER YOU SOLD THE SUPERGUN TO A GULF STATE?

I'M AFRAID THAT'S CLASSIFIED INFORMATION.

BUT YOU DID DESIGN A GUN WITH A HALF-MILE LONG BARREL INTENDED TO LOB TACTICAL NUCLEAR DEVICES SOME FOUR HUNDRED MILES?

I WOULD LIKE TO BE ABLE TO COMMENT, BUT I'M UNDER RESTRICTIONS ON THAT SUBJECT.

I SEE. HOW MANY OF THESE DEVICES LED YOU TO THE DESIGN OF THE "IRON MAN" SUIT?

I THINK EVERYTHING WAS LEADING ME TOWARDS THE IRON MAN.

IS IT A MILITARY DEVICE?

I DON'T THINK SO.

BUT, IN KEEPING WITH YOUR OTHER INVENTIONS, IT CERTAINLY HAS MILITARY APPLICATIONS?

EVERYTHING HAS MILITARY APPLICATIONS. ALL TOOLS HAVE A DESTRUCTIVE POTENTIAL.

LASER ARRAY FOR RECORDING SOUND OFF WINDOW GLASS VIP

AND THE IRON MAN SUIT CERTAINLY POSSESSES AWESOME DESTRUCTIVE POTENTIAL, DOESN'T IT?

I MEAN, I DON'T SEE A BENIGN SIDE TO YOUR PATENTED "REPULSOR" TECHNOLOGY.

ACTUALLY, THE REPULSOR HAS APPLICATION TO CHEAP, NON-CHEMICAL SPACELAUNCH.

I SEE. AND ARE YOU DEVELOPING THAT?

...NOT AT THIS TIME.

I BELIEVE THE UNKNOWN TEST PILOT OF THE IRON MAN SUIT IS IN FACT TASKED SOLELY AS YOUR PERSONAL BODYGUARD.

I SEE.

THAT'S A LITTLE DISINGENUOUS OF YOU, JOHN.

YOU'RE WELL AWARE THAT I DONATE IRON MAN'S SERVICES TO SPECIAL RESPONSE GROUPS LIKE THE AVENGERS ALL THE TIME.

SURE. MY POINT IS THAT, OTHER THAN GUARDING YOU AND PERFORMING PEACEKEEPING OPERATIONS...

...WELL, THE IRON MAN SUIT ISN'T USED FOR ANYTHING ELSE. THEREFORE, REALLY, IT'S JUST A DEFENSE INDUSTRY APPLICATION, RIGHT?

ALL TECHNOLOGIES HAVE THAT KIND OF APPLICATION.

MY POINT--AND I DON'T WANT TO TALK OVER YOU, JOHN, BUT YOU'VE RUN ME OVER WHENEVER I'VE TRIED TO EXPAND ON AN ANSWER--

--MY *POINT*, JOHN, IS THAT STARK MICROELECTRONIC BREAKTHROUGHS HAVE ALL LED TO USEFUL SOCIAL TECHNOLOGIES THROUGH THAT INITIAL MILITARY FUNDING.

NO, I DIDN'T FIRST THINK TO MYSELF THAT TAKING MICROCHIPS DOWN TO THE NANOMETER LIMIT WOULD BE GOOD FOR BOMBS.

AND THE MONEY FROM SEEDPOD WAS DRIVEN INTO MEDICAL BIOMETRIC IMPLANTS, CARDIAC REPLACEMENT MEDICINE AND INTERNAL ANALGESIC PUMPS.

AM I AN ARMS DEALER? NO. DID I START OUT AS A WEAPONS DESIGNER? YES. DO I INTEND TO DIE AS ONE? NO.

DO YOU THINK THEY HAVE YOUR PAINKILLING DRUG PUMPS IN IRAQ?

DO YOU THINK AN AFGHAN KID WITH HIS ARMS BLOWN OFF BY A LANDMINE IS REMOTELY IMPRESSED BY AN IRON MAN SUIT?

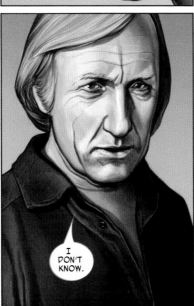

MR. STARK, SINCE YOU'VE REJOINED THE LIVING, I'VE SCHEDULED A SENIOR STAFF MEETING FOR--

CANCEL IT.

I'M GOING BACK DOWN TO THE GARAGE.

--NO, GEOFF, WE'LL TALK ABOUT THE INTERVIEW LATER.

I'M WELL AWARE THAT BILL STEPPED DOWN AS CEO OF MICROSOFT AND TOOK A "CHIEF TECHNOLOGIST" TITLE--

--ALL RIGHT. SENIOR STAFF AT FOUR. BUT NOW I NEED TO BE IN THE GARAGE.

STARK VOICELOG: RECORD: DATESTAMP.

JOHN PILLINGER SAYS THE IRON MAN SUIT IS A MILITARY APPLICATION.

I TOLD HIM HE WAS WRONG. I'M TRYING TO DECIDE IF I WAS LYING.

I'VE NEVER SOLD ANY ELEMENT OF THE IRON MAN TO THE MILITARY.

IT'S USED FOR EXTRAORDINARY RESCUE AND RESPONSE SITUATIONS.

IRON MAN SAVES LIVES.

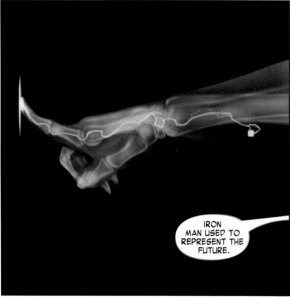

IRON MAN USED TO REPRESENT THE FUTURE.

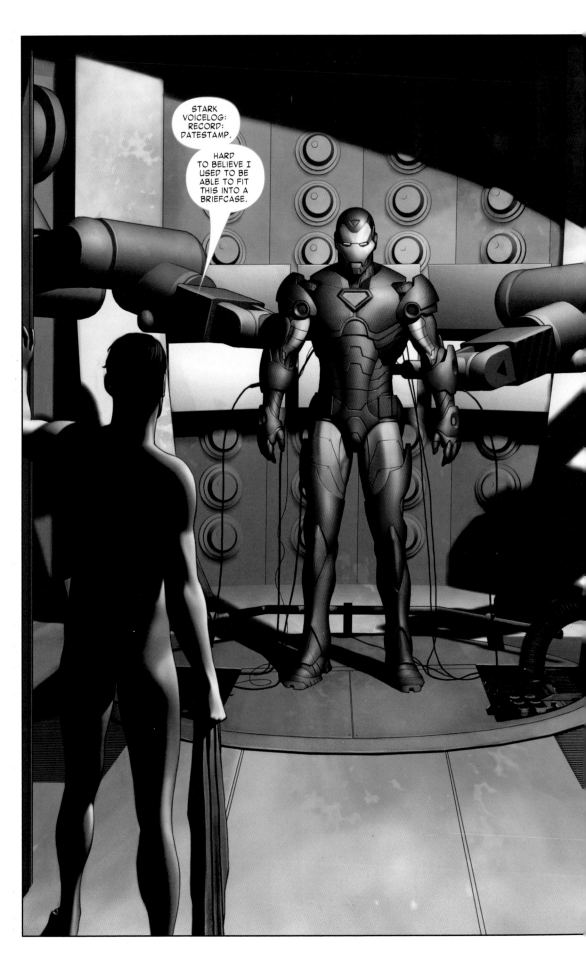

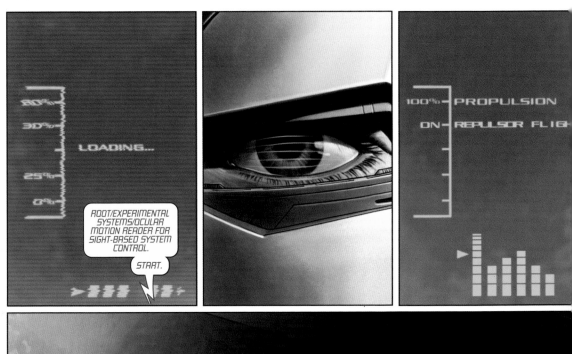

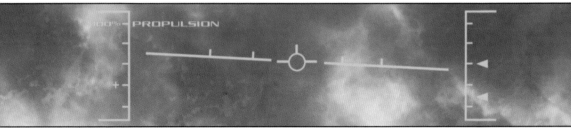

OFF—PROPULSION
ON—REPULSOR FLIGHT SYSTEM

BARELY OUT OF YOUR TWENTIES. IN A SUIT AT AN EMERGENT TECH CONFERENCE. COMPLAINING ABOUT CONSUMER SOCIETY.

AND YOU GOT YOUR MONEY FROM THE MILITARY.

YOU KNOW WHO I AM?

EVERYONE HERE KNOWS WHO YOU ARE.

HUH. I THINK YOU'RE THE FIRST PERSON WHO'S SAID TWO WORDS TO ME.

THEY'RE *TERRIFIED* OF YOU.

YOU REINVENTED MICROTECHNOLOGY IN YOUR DAD'S GARAGE. YOUR BRAIN IS LIKE THREE FEET OVER THE HEADS OF EVERYONE ELSE HERE.

YOU'RE TONY STARK. I'M MAYA HANSEN.

THE MEDICAL DESIGNER? REPROGRAMMING THE REPAIR CENTER?

RIGHT.

HEY. SAL KENNEDY'S ABOUT TO TALK. YOU WANT TO COME SEE IT WITH ME?

WHO'S HE?

KENNEDY? STARTED OUT AS A COMPUTER GUY, BECAME AN ETHNOBOTANIST, WORKS AS A FUTURIST NOW.

SOUNDS LIKE IT'D AT LEAST BE INTERESTING.

SO COME ON.

AND LOOSEN YOUR TIE.

TONY STARK'S OFFICE, PLEASE.

NO, TELL HIM IT'S MAYA HANSEN, AND REMIND HIM OF THE LOUSY PUB DEAL AT TECHWEST.

THE LOUSY PUB AT TECHWEST?

WHERE WE PROMISED WE'D ALWAYS TAKE EACH OTHER'S CALLS AND IMS.

OVER BEER WE WERE CONVINCED SOMEONE ELSE HAD ALREADY DIGESTED AND PASSED.

TONY, I REALLY NEED SOMEONE TO TALK TO.

SOMETHING'S HAPPENED HERE, AND...WELL, IT FEELS LIKE THE LAST STRAW.

WHERE ARE YOU, MAYA?

FUTUREPHARM. THE MAIN LABS, OUTSIDE AUSTIN.

YOU'RE SURE?

I'M HEADED OUT TO MY PRIVATE JET NOW. I'LL SEE YOU IN A FEW HOURS.

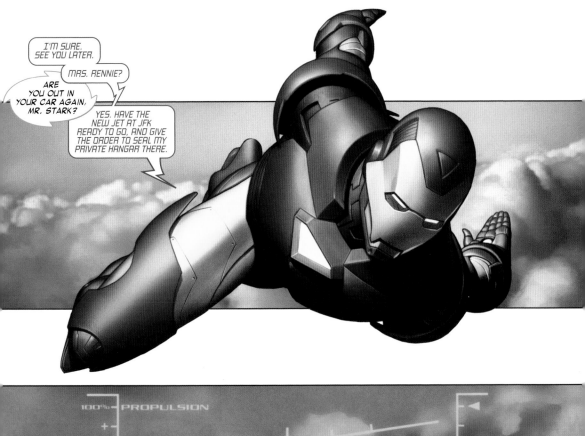

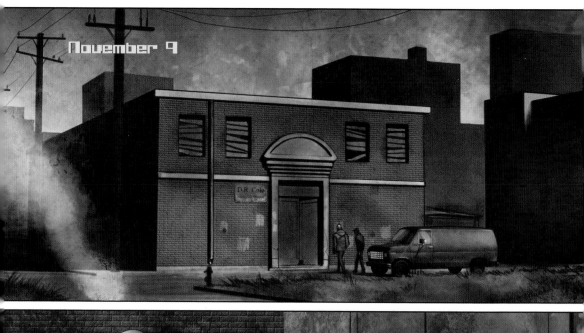

November 9

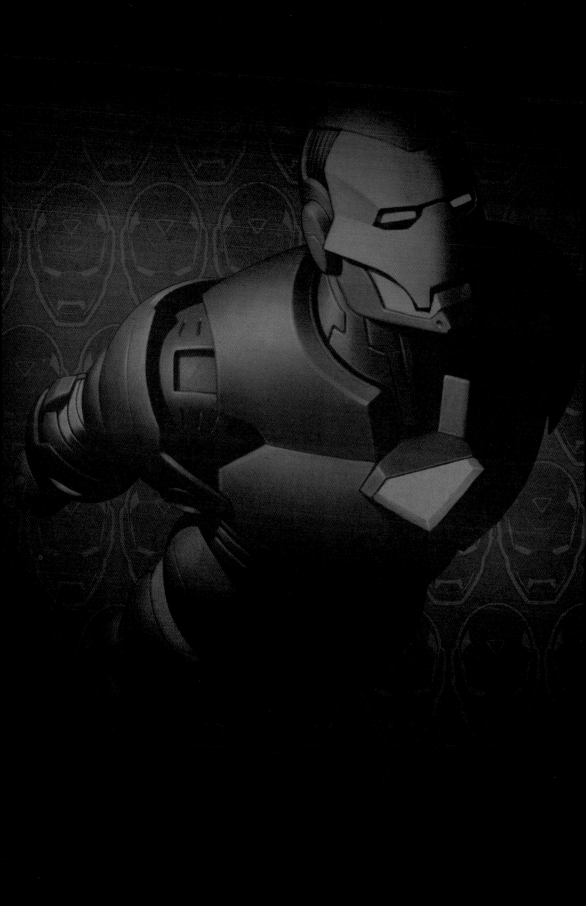

Iron Man

Written by Warren Ellis
Illustrated by Adi Granov

"Extremis"

STARK INTERNATIONAL

Lettering by UC's Randy Gentile
Assistant Editors: Schmidt, Wiley & Lazer
Editor: Tom Brevoort
Editor in Chief: Joe Quesada
Publisher: Dan Buckley

WE HAD THE NEW HANDSET COURIERED TO YOUR PLANE. YOU HAVE IT THERE?

YEAH, GEOFF, LISTEN, I HAVE NOTES ON AN OCULAR CONTROL SYSTEM.

TONY...

IT'S A SPRAY OF VERY LOW-POWER LASERS THAT READ CHANGES OF MOTION AND PRESSURE IN THE EYE. BASICALLY, IT CAN TELL WHAT YOU'RE LOOKING AT.

THE PHONE, TONY.

YEAH. THIS IS THE STARK 99?

STARK INTERNATIONAL

S.H.I.E.L.D.'S AN INTERNATIONAL ORGANIZATION. IT'S DIFFERENT.

WE'VE JUST INVENTED THE BEST CELL PHONE ON EARTH. WE DON'T NEED MILITARY MONEY ANYMORE.

TONY, WE'RE HIP-DEEP IN RESEARCH AND DEVELOPMENT ON THIRTY DIFFERENT THINGS, EIGHTY PERCENT OF WHICH WON'T REALIZE ANY MONEY IN THE NEXT THREE YEARS.

MILITARY MONEY IS THE EASIEST WAY TO IMPROVE CASH FLOW.

I MEAN, WE COULD LICENSE TECHNOLOGIES ELSEWHERE. BUT WE NEED YOU TO SIGN OFF ON THOSE.

AND WHEN YOU SPEND SIX WEEKS IN THE GARAGE...

IF YOU WANT TO MAKE THE WORLD A BETTER PLACE, YOU HAVE TO LET SOMEONE HELP YOU.

FUTUREPHARM

MAYA...

WALKED RIGHT INTO THE OFFICE, AND THERE HE WAS...

WHOA, WHOA.

MY PROJECT DIRECTOR KILLED HIMSELF AND-- DAMMIT--

HE STOLE MY PROJECT AND GAVE IT TO SOMEONE, AND WE DON'T KNOW WHO.

SHOW ME HIS OFFICE.

THE POLICE HAVE BEEN AND GONE. THEY SAID THEY'RE SENDING ANOTHER TEAM TO PICK IT UP.

THE COMPUTER'S STILL HERE?

WE CAN'T BREAK ITS SECURITY.

HM. THE PROJECT-- WAS IT YOUR FIELD?

BIOELECTRICS, ROBOTIC MICROSURGERY.

MARKKO. TONY STARK. I NEED A FAVOR.

I'M GOING TO SEND YOU AN ENTIRE COMPUTER HARD DRIVE VIA ZIPSAT, OKAY? I NEED IT CRACKED.

YEAH. STAND BY.

ZIPSAT?

MY OWN CONSTELLATION OF SATELLITES PROVIDING WIRELESS BROADBAND INTERNET.

YOU KNOW, THE PAPERS CALL YOU A LADIES' MAN, BUT I REALLY CAN'T IMAGINE THAT MAKES GIRLS LAY DOWN...

IT MAKES ME LOTS OF MONEY. I USUALLY FIND THAT DOES THE TRICK.

THERE.

CLASSY WOMEN YOU KNOW.

EXTREMELY.

YOU KNOW WHAT? LET'S GO SEE SAL.

YOU THINK?

HE'S STILL IN THE BAY AREA, RIGHT? SAL ALWAYS MAKES YOU FEEL BETTER. AND YOU DON'T WANT TO BE AROUND HERE.

I DON'T KNOW. I DON'T FEEL LIKE PACKING.

PACKING, HELL. MY PLANE'S ON STANDBY AND I'LL HAVE A CAR WAITING AT SFA.

I HAVE A VERY FAST PLANE. YOU'LL BE BACK HERE FOR DINNER. LET'S GET YOU OUT OF HERE FOR A WHILE.

YOU HAVE A PLANE.

PLANES. SIMILAR TO THE QUINJET DESIGN I GAVE TO THE AVENGERS. ONLY, YOU KNOW, FASTER.

YOU ARE SO WEIRD.

Bastrop, Tx

To Houston, Tx: 190 Miles

FBI Houston Division

NOT ME.

I DON'T TOUCH IT ANYMORE. MAKES ME SLEEPY.

MY CHILDREN HAVE BECOME WEENIE STRAIGHT PEOPLE. THE HORROR.

COME THROUGH, COME THROUGH. I JUST PRESSED SOME APPLE JUICE.

SIT, SIT.

I KNOW IT DOESN'T LOOK LIKE MUCH TO YOU MILITARY/INDUSTRIAL-FUNDED TYPES, BUT IT SUITS ME NOW.

I'M SOLO, SAL. AND MAYA'S SALARIED BY AN INDEPENDENT--

YES, YOU'RE BOTH WORKING FOR THE MILITARY. FOR CORPORATIONS. FOR THE GOVERNMENT.

YOU FAIL TO SEE THAT THEY ARE ALL THE SAME THING.

THESE ARE INESCAPABLE TRUTHS. YOU CANNOT DO THE SCIENCE YOU WANT WITHOUT STEPPING INTO THEIR POOL.

I DO A WHOLE RAP ABOUT THIS AT ESALEN IN THE SUMMERTIME, YOU KNOW. UNDER THE TEACHING TREE.

THE TEACHING TREE.

YEAH, I KNOW.

TECH PEOPLE GO OUT THERE TOO. THERE'S ONE GUY WHO BELIEVES ALL TECHNOLOGICAL INNOVATION WORK SHOULD BE DONE "FROM THE HEART."

HE TAKES HIS CODEMONKEYS OUT THERE AND MAKES THEM DO YOGA 'TIL THEY PUKE.

IT "GETS THE HEART CENTER WORKING."

THIS IS THE PROBLEM WITH THINKING AT THIS LEVEL. THE BASIC TRUTHS--THAT AMERICA IS NOW BEING RUN AS A POST-POLITICAL CORPORATE CONGLOMERATE--ARE TOO BITTER TO SWALLOW.

IT'S EASIER FOR HALF-SMART PEOPLE TO THINK THE PATH TO FREEDOM REQUIRES YOU TO STAND ON ONE LEG FOR AN HOUR.

WE'RE FACING UP TO THE FUTURE. BUT WE CAN'T SEE IT. I ALWAYS THOUGHT IT'D BE YOU TWO WHO'D BE ROAD TESTING THE FUTURE FOR US.

BUT YOU, YOU'RE STUCK IN ESSENTIALLY PUNCHING *BIOLOGICAL* STRUCTURE UNTIL IT GIVES UP AND DOES WHAT YOU WANT.

AND TONY, YOU'VE FIDDLED WITH SOME MEDICAL PATENTS AND BUILT A SUPER HERO SUIT.

SHE'S THE EDWARD TELLER OF BIOLOGY AND YOU'RE THE DEAN KAMEN OF TECHNOLOGY.

THAT'S NOT FAIR. DEAN KAMEN'S DONE GOOD, USEFUL WORK.

YEAH, BUT HE ALSO MADE THE SEGWAY.

CLIVE SINCLAIR MADE BRITAIN A CENTER OF EXCELLENCE FOR CONSUMER MICROCOMPUTING, BUT ALL HE'S REMEMBERED FOR IS THE C5, WHICH WAS A SEGWAY WITH PEDALS.

YOU TWO ARE GOING TO YOUR GRAVES WITH THE EPITAPH "ALMOST USEFUL."

BUT THEN, SO AM I.

WHAT ARE YOU WORKING ON RIGHT NOW?

MOSTLY, I'M TAKING DRUGS. I SPEND MY DAYS COOKING DOWN ILLINOIS BUNDLEWEED INTO DMT AND RAISING MUSHROOMS.

YOU AND YOUR DAMN PSYCHEDELICS.

YOU NEVER WOULD DROP LSD, WOULD YOU?

I LIKED WHISKY BETTER.

GOOD FOR YOU. I'VE COME TO CONSIDER LSD AS ABRASIVELY PSYCHIATRIC.

IT REALLY JUST RERUNS ALL YOUR MEMORY STORES AT RANDOM. DMT AND MUSHROOMS ARE MUCH MORE INTERESTING AND ALIVE.

DRUGS ARE TECHNOLOGIES, TONY.

IN THE PLACES WHERE HUMANITY FIRST AROSE, THERE WERE PSYCHEDELIC MUSHROOMS. IT'S A MEDICAL FACT THAT THOSE MUSHROOMS IMPROVE VISUAL ACUITY.

THAT WOULD MAKE EARLY HUMANS BETTER HUNTERS.

THE IRON MAN SUIT YOU BUILT, TONY--IT HAS SENSORS, ZOOM LENSES AND THE LIKE?

YES.

SAME THING. WHATEVER POOR MORON YOU STUFF INTO THAT SUIT CAN SEE BETTER. SAME WITH EARLY HUMANS WHO HAD MUSHROOMS IN THEIR DIET.

I IMAGINE YOUR EXTREMIS PROCESS REDESIGNED THE HUMAN EYE, TOO.

YEAH.

AND YOU WERE BOTH IN THE BUSINESS OF MAKING BETTER HUNTERS. HAVEN'T STRAYED FAR FROM THE PACK, HAVE YOU?

WHY ARE YOU BOTH HERE?

ADVICE.

AH. COME TO SEE THE WISE MAN OF THE FOREST. THE OLD SHAMAN.

YOU KNOW WHAT THEY CALL A SHAMAN IN AUSTRALIA?

THE CLEVER FELLA.

WHICH ONE OF YOU IS IN TROUBLE?

THAT WOULD BE ME.

LET ME GUESS. THE OLD SUPER-SOLDIER THING. THAT'S ALWAYS BUGGED YOU. MICROELECTRONIC PLUG-INS FOR THE BRAIN?

YEAH.

Y'KNOW, NO ONE'S EVER GOTTEN A RESULT EXACTLY LIKE OLD ERSKINE DID WITH CAPTAIN AMERICA.

YOU KNOW WHAT A HIERONYMUS MACHINE IS?

IT'S A BUNCH OF JUNK IN A BOX. IT JUST HAPPENS TO WORK EXACTLY TO THE EXPERIMENTER'S INTENT.

SOME PEOPLE THINK THAT ERSKINE'S FORMULA WAS A HIERONYMUS MACHINE--THAT IT WAS SIMPLY HIS OWN FORCE OF WILL THAT MADE IT WORK EXACTLY LIKE A PERFECT SUPER-SOLDIER DOSE.

YOU'RE BOTH IN TROUBLE. IT'S JUST THAT HE DOESN'T KNOW IT YET.

YOU CAN BARELY LOOK AT YOURSELF IN THE MIRROR, CAN YOU, TONY?

YOU'RE RICH NOW. INDEPENDENT. I HAVE A FEELING YOU DO GOOD WORKS, WHEN YOU CAN.

BUT IT'S NOT ENOUGH.

YOU HAVE INTELLECT AND POWER, BUT IT'S NOT ENOUGH. IT'S LIKE THERE'S A DAM ACROSS YOUR LIFE.

HER PROBLEM IS THAT SHE'S A WOMAN. THERE'S A GLASS CEILING. IT COULD TAKE HER ANOTHER FIVE, TEN YEARS TO GET TO WHERE YOU ARE NOW.

AND WHAT WOULD YOU DO WHEN YOU GOT TO TONY'S POSITION?

FOUR YEARS OF ENGINEERING AND I COULD CURE CANCER.

THERE YOU GO.

AND WHAT DO YOU THINK OF AT NIGHT, TONY?

...MAKING A BETTER IRON MAN SUIT.

SO THAT YOUR POOR BODYGUARD CAN WRESTLE MONSTERS OR WHATEVER IT IS HE DOES?

NO. AND YOUR JUICE STINKS.

SO WHAT DOES HE DO ASIDE FROM BEATING UP FIN FANG FOOM?

WOULD THE IRON MAN SUIT END WAR?

IT'D BE HARD TO KILL SOMEONE IN AN IRON MAN SUIT.

FOR A YEAR. UNTIL THE SUIT'S SPECS WERE SUPERCEDED. IF THEY HAVEN'T BEEN ALREADY.

PERHAPS BY HER.

AND A *SUIT*, TONY. IS THAT ALL IT CAN BE?

SHE'S WORKING ON MILITARY APPS BECAUSE THAT'S HOW SHE'S GOING TO GET THE FUNDING AND THE SPACE TO CURE DISEASE. WHAT ABOUT YOU?

WHAT'S THE IRON MAN *FOR*, TONY?

I TRIED TO INCULCATE IN BOTH OF YOU A SENSE OF THE FUTURE.

RIGHT FROM TECHWEST. YOU REMEMBER THAT? YOU TURNED UP DRUNK, AND HE TURNED UP IN A SUIT.

BUT YOU BOTH HAD THE FUTURE IN YOU.

WHY AREN'T YOU RUNNING THE TABLE?

SORRY. PHONE.

HATE HOSE.

SAL, CAN YOU PUT ON CNN?

OH, FOR...

I DON'T HAVE A TV.

HOLD ON. THERE'S A TV TUNER ON MY PHONE.

BREAKING NEWS

CNN

STARK

BREAKING NEWS

ST

YEAH, I'M STILL HERE.

TONY, CAN YOU TURN UP THE SOUND?

...FEW SURVIVORS WE SPOKE TO INDICATE A SINGLE UNARMED MAN DID ALL THIS--

--DISABLING THE ELEVATORS AND TORCHING THE GROUND LEVEL, TRAPPING THE BUILDING'S STAFF IN A RISING BLAZE--

CNN

BREAKING NEW

--AND LEAVING THE LIVING AND THE DEAD TO BE INCINERATED IN THE LOBBY.

ALMOST SURREAL SCENES OF--OH, GOD, MOVE THE CAMERA, I'M SORRY--

HE WAS, HE WAS BREATHING FIRE, YOU COULD SEE THE RIPPLE OF GAS COMING OUT OF HIS THROAT--

--AND, AND THEN HE CAME BACK, AND THINGS CAME OUT OF HIS HANDS--

RECORDED EARLIE

WHY ARE WE WATCHING THIS, MAYA?

THE SIGNATURES.

THE FIRE. THE HANDS. A FEW OTHER THINGS.

AN EXTREMIS ENHANCILE DID THIS.

WHOEVER STOLE THE EXTREMIS DOSE TOOK IT, TONY. AND LIVED.

AND DID THIS.

THIS IS STARK. BRING THE LIMO AROUND. PREP THE PLANE FOR IMMEDIATE RETURN TO AUSTIN.

AND TELL MRS. RENNIE I WANT MY CAR FLOWN TO AUSTIN ON THE SISTER PLANE, IMMEDIATELY. IN ITS CRATE.

WHAT DID YOU DO, MADDEN?

WHAT DID I DO? I JUST STARTED.

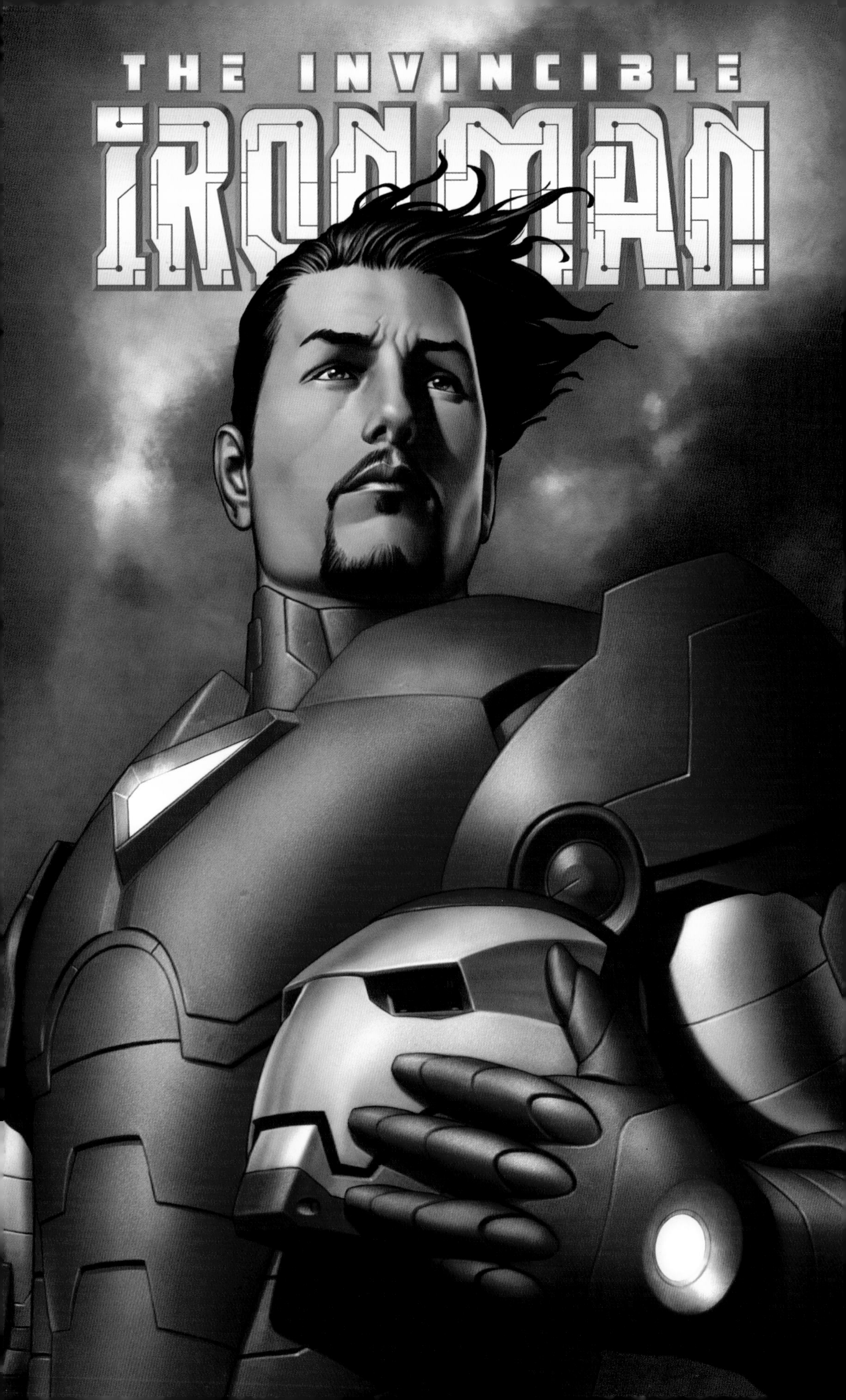
THE INVINCIBLE
IRON MAN

Iron Man

Written by Warren Ellis
Illustrated by Adi Granov

"Extremis"

Lettering by VC's Randy Gentile
Assistant Editors: Schmidt, Moore and Lazer
Editor: Tom Brevoort

HOW CAN YOU BE SURE?

ASIDE FROM THE CLEAR SIGNATURES AND THE COMPUTER ANALYSIS ON THE VIDEO REPORT THAT MY STAFF PERFORMED?

IT HAPPENED WITHIN DRIVING DISTANCE OF US, INSIDE A COUPLE OF DAYS OF A SUCCESSFUL EXTREMIS INSTALLATION PERIOD.

Three of Six

Editor in chief: Joe Quesada
Publisher: Dan Buckley

EXTREMIS.

I THINK IT'S TIME YOU TOLD ME ABOUT EXTREMIS.

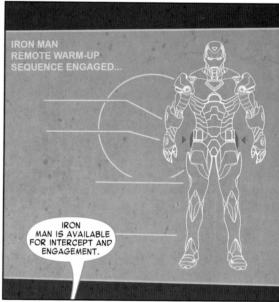

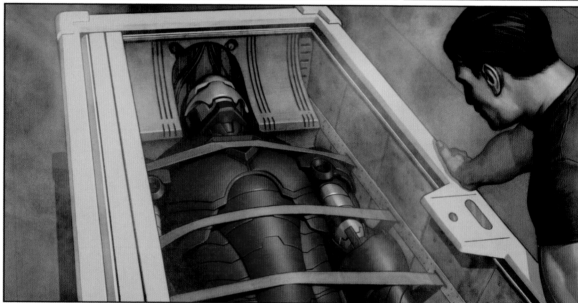

I MUST BE CRAZY.

OKAY. FOR MY NEXT TRICK: SNEAKING OUT OF A HANGAR AND LAUNCHING WITHOUT ANYONE NOTICING.

I TRY TO BUY THE MORE REMOTE HANGARS, BUT THERE'S ALWAYS SOME KID WITH A DIGITAL CAMERA.

USUALLY A STARK CAMERA.

NO. FOR MY NEXT TRICK: LOCKING THE DAMN DOOR SO NO ONE ACCIDENTALLY GETS TO SEE IRON MAN BUTT NAKED.

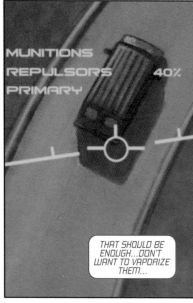

MUNITIONS
REPULSORS
PRIMARY 40%

THAT SHOULD BE
ENOUGH...DON'T
WANT TO VAPORIZE
THEM...

DAMN, HE'S FAST--

RESPONSE SERVERS   100%

RESTART

OH, GOD.

MUNITIONS
SCREAMERS / 4SECS

IIIIIEEEEEEEIIIIIIEEEEE

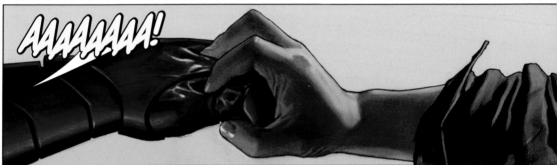

AAAAAAAA!

TORSO UNIT BREACH

Iron Man

Written by Warren Ellis
Illustrated by Adi Granov

"Extremis"

Lettering by VC's Randy Gentile
Assistant Editors: Schmidt, Sitterson and Lazer
Editor: Tom Brevoort

Four of Six

Editor in Chief: Joe Quesada
Publisher: Dan Buckley

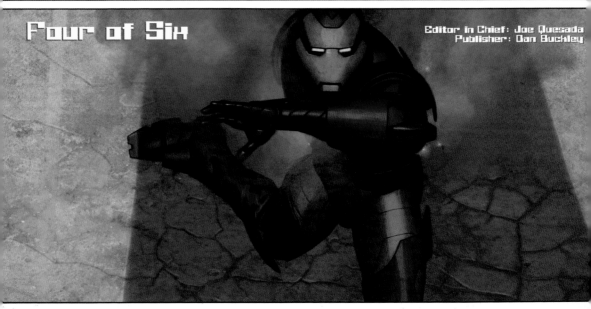

POWER TRANSMISSION 0%

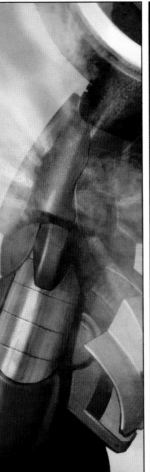

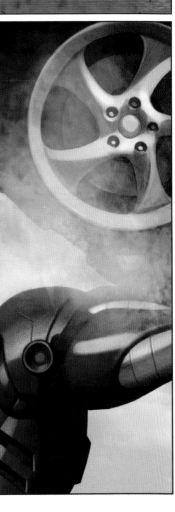

UFFF

OWW. YOU BASTARD....

DOESN'T MATTER. NOT IMPORTANT.

I HAVE ALL THE TIME IN THE WORLD NOW.

LEAVE THE LITTLE THINGS BEHIND.

AUXILIARY POWER ON/IRON MAN SAFE MODE

COME ON, COME ON... GIVE ME THE SECONDARY SYSTEMS.

MOMMY, MOMMY, THE FIRES ARE COMING THIS WAY--

I KNOW THE DOORS WON'T OPEN OH GOD OH GOD!

THERMOCOUPLE/HEAT-INDUCTIVE TRANSFER FIELD

HEAT-POWER TRANSFER SUCCESSFUL
POWER AT 1%

I DON'T *FEEL* VERY SUCCESSFUL...

IRON MAN TO ALL POINTS: I'M GOING TO BE *IMMOBILIZED* IN ABOUT A MINUTE AND A HALF.

COUGH

COULD USE SOME *COUGH* HELP.

MEDICAL/SUIT EMERGENCY INTERVENTION SYSTEM AUTO-ACTIVATING
SEEK URGENT MEDICAL ASSISTANCE

WELL, THAT'S A HELP.

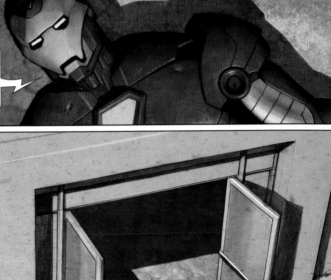

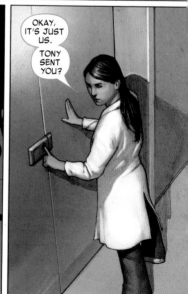

HE'S A BIOLOGICAL COMBAT MACHINE...AND I'M JUST A MAN IN AN IRON SUIT.

I'VE SPENT MONTHS IN MY GARAGE TRYING TO INCREASE THE ARMOR'S RESPONSE TIME. AND IT'S STILL. NOT. FAST. ENOUGH.

I NEED TO WIRE THE ARMOR DIRECTLY INTO MY BRAIN. EXTREMIS COULD DO THAT.

MAYBE WE COULD WORK IN SOME KIND OF TIVO THING WHILE WE'RE AT IT. MY COMPANY BOARD WOULD LOVE BRAIN TELEVISION.

EXTREMIS IS UNTESTED EVEN IN ITS CURRENT CONFIGURATION--

SEEMS TO WORK FINE. JUST LOOK AT MY FACE.

--AND THE GUY WAS PRESUMABLY HEALTHY WHEN HE TOOK THE DOSE. YOU LOOK LIKE YOU'VE BEEN PUSHED THROUGH A WOODCHIPPER.

GAK!

EXTREMIS WORKS THROUGH THE HEALING CENTER, YOU SAID.

IT'LL FIX ME WHILE IT'S WORKING.

I DON'T NEED THE POWERS. IF ANYTHING, WE'RE TALKING ABOUT SIMPLIFYING THE PAYLOAD.

I NEED TO BE THE SUIT. INSTEAD OF GROWING NEW ORGANS...I NEED TO GROW NEW CONNECTIONS...

THIS THING'S GOTTEN TOO HEAVY. AND TOO SLOW.

I'M TALKING ABOUT SPEED OF DEPLOYMENT... SPEED OF OPERATION...

TONY...

THANK GOD FOR PAINKILLERS, EH?

GET A COMPUTER IN HERE...

WELL, IT WILL BE.

BZZT!

EXCUSE ME.

MAYA HANSEN.

OH. I'LL BE RIGHT THERE.

HOW MUCH DO YOU SPEND ON PLANES? A PACKAGE FROM CONEY ISLAND HAS ARRIVED FOR YOU.

I'LL BE RIGHT BACK. MAKE YOURSELF... COMFORTABLE, I GUESS.

ONE OF THE ITEMS WILL BE A CASE. BRING IT BACK?

Iron Man Hud Playback

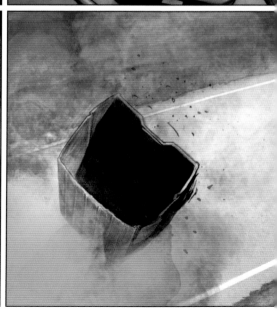

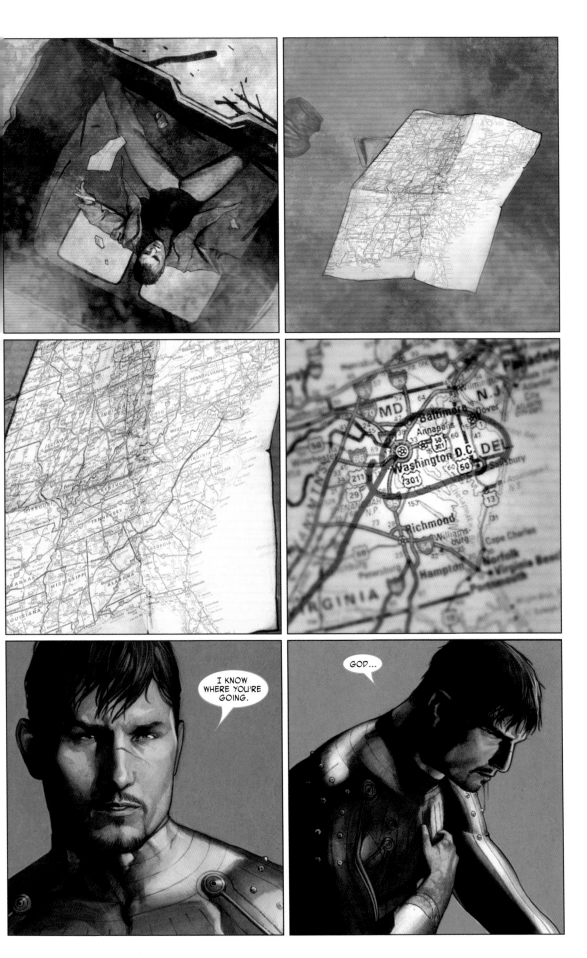

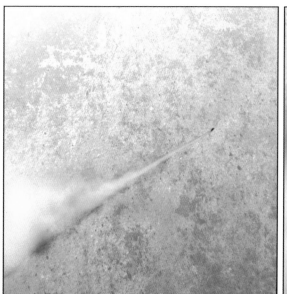

IS THAT HOW YOU SEE AMERICA?

SURE.

YOU KNOW, THE KLAN DID GOOD THINGS TOO. THEY DEFENDED CHRISTIAN LAW IN A LOT OF PLACES.

I'M SO SICK OF HEARING ABOUT GOD ALL THE TIME. I'M SICK OF HAVING TO, LIKE, PASS A RELIGIOUS TEST JUST TO LIVE HERE.

THE KLAN LYNCHED PEOPLE WHO DIDN'T LOOK LIKE REGULAR WHITE FOLKS.

REGULAR WHITE FOLKS BUILT THIS COUNTRY. WITHOUT GOVERNMENT OR SPIES OR REGULATIONS OR PEOPLE WITH BADGES WHO KILL YOUR FAMILY FOR FUN.

YEAH. EXCEPT REGULAR WHITE FOLKS DID ALL THAT TOO.

DON'T SAY THAT. IT ALL WENT WRONG. I'M GOING TO FIX IT.

I'VE GOT THIS STUFF INSIDE ME, SEE? FROM THE FUTURE THEY WERE GOING TO MAKE. AND I'M USING IT TO TURN BACK THE CLOCK.

BACK TO LYNCHINGS AND GIVING SMALLPOX-INFECTED BLANKETS TO THE DIFFERENT-LOOKING PEOPLE?

YOU'RE AS BAD AS THEM. LEAVE ME ALONE.

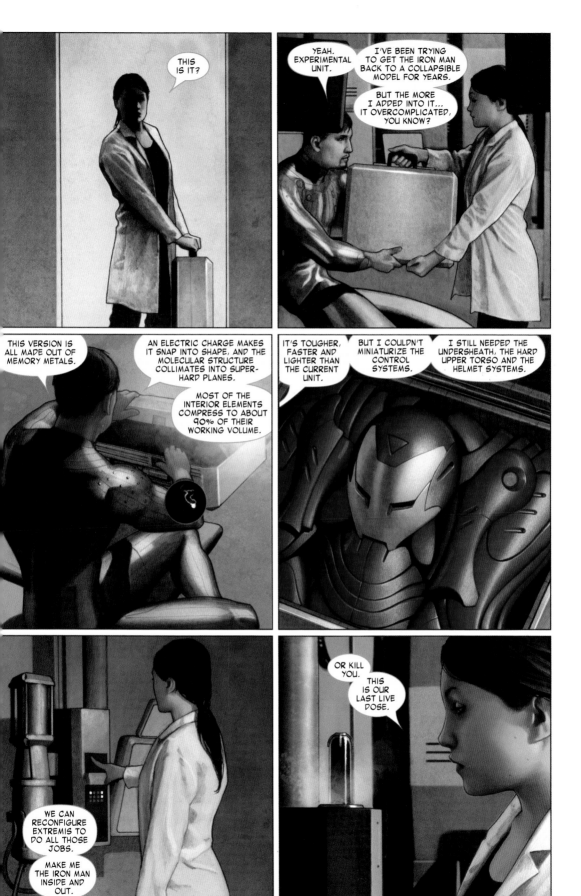

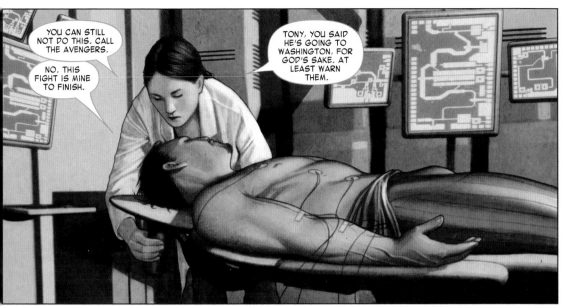

BUT I ALWAYS WANTED TO BE MORE. SAL SAID SOMETHING ABOUT BENCH-TESTING THE FUTURE?

TEST PILOT FOR THE FUTURE.

FUNNY: THIS IS THE SECOND TIME I'VE HAD TO WORK AGAINST THE CLOCK FOR THE IRON MAN TO SAVE MY LIFE.

KK
KKKAHHKK

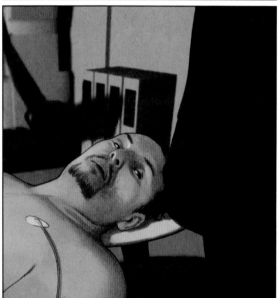

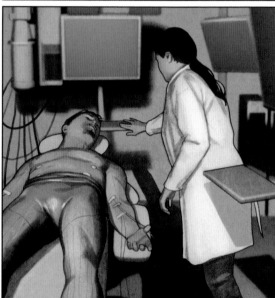

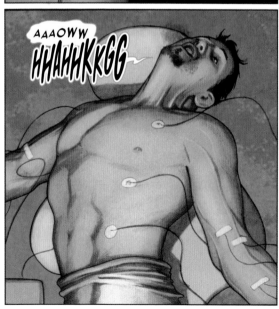

AAAOWW
HHAHHKKGG

HRUP

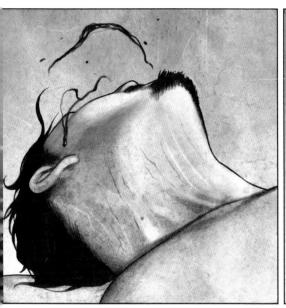

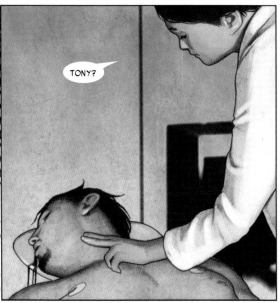

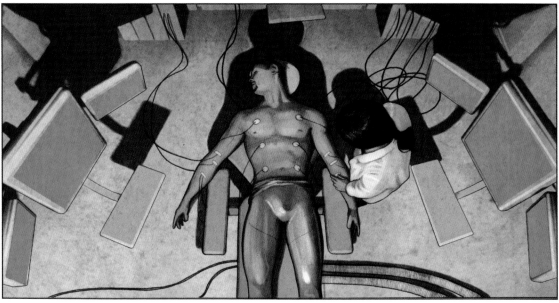

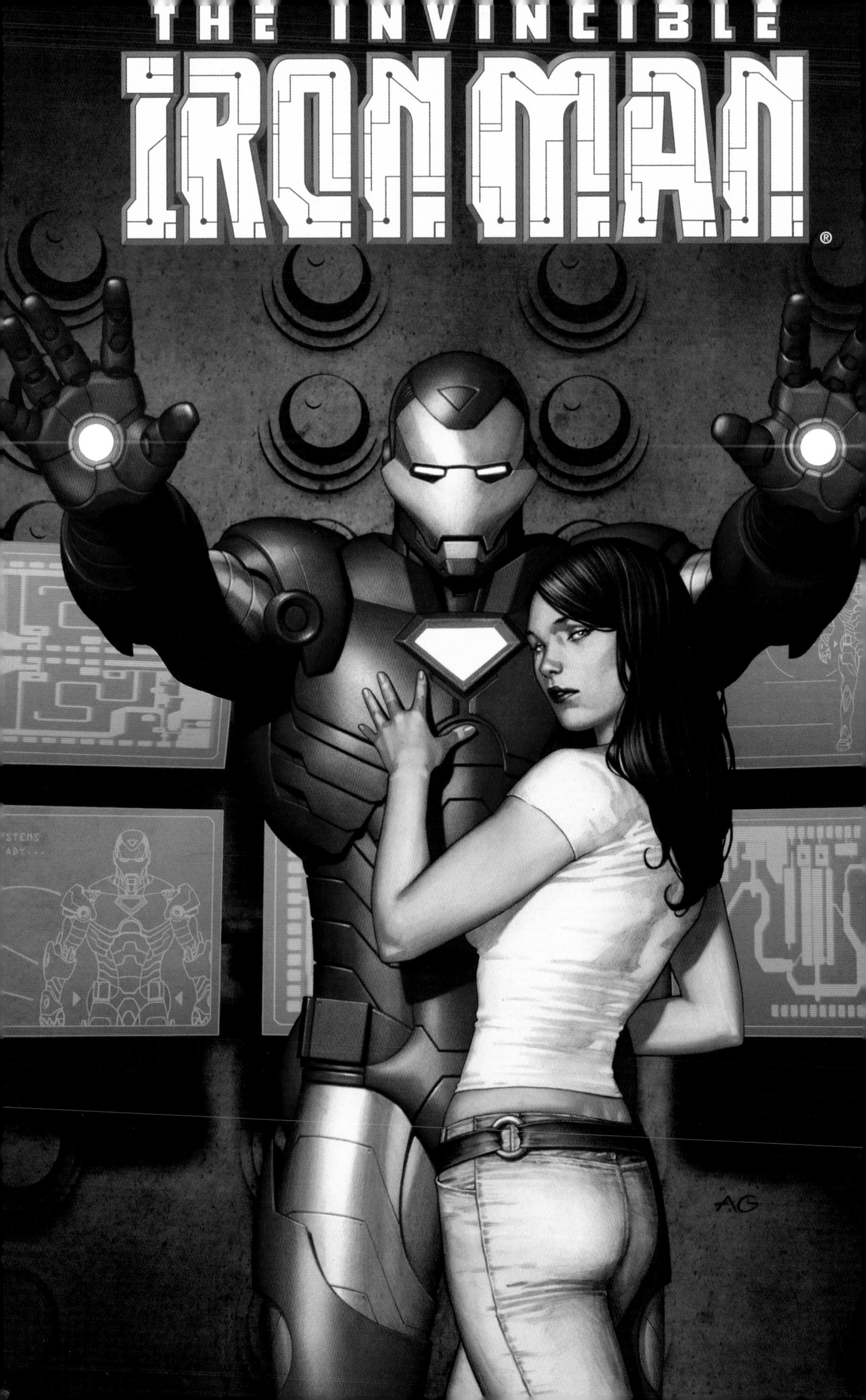
THE INVINCIBLE
IRON MAN®

OH, GOD.

I'M STILL CONSCIOUS.

Extremis"

Lettering By: Vc's Randy Gentile
Assistant Editors: Schmidt, Lazer & Sitterson
Editor: Tom Brevoort

WHAT'S HAPPENING? MAYA?

MAYA, SOMETHING'S GONE WRONG. CAN YOU HEAR ME?

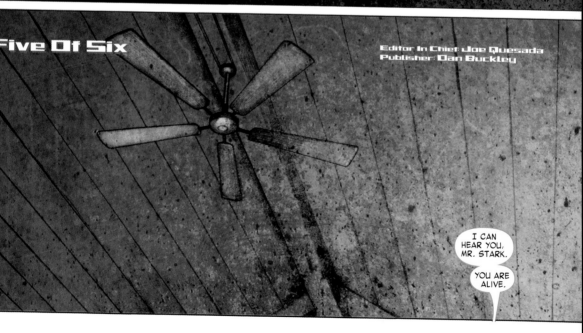

Editor In Chief: Joe Quesada
Publisher: Dan Buckley

I CAN HEAR YOU, MR. STARK.

YOU ARE ALIVE.

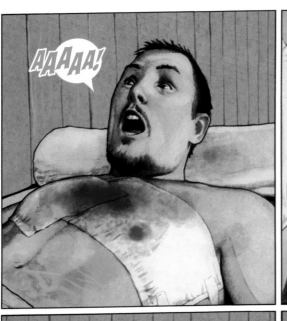

AAAAA!

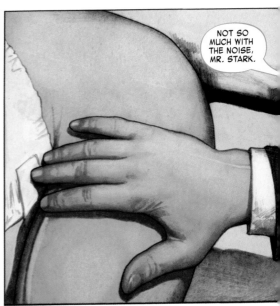

NOT SO MUCH WITH THE NOISE, MR. STARK.

AND NOT SO MUCH WITH THE MOVING.

THERE IS A PIECE OF SHRAPNEL LODGED NEXT TO YOUR HEART. I COULD NOT REMOVE IT.

I KNOW YOU. WE MET AT A CONFERENCE...

HO YINSEN. THE MEDICAL FUTURIST.

GOOD MEMORY FOR ONE WHO WAS SO BLISTERINGLY DRUNK.

I GOT TOO USED TO THE EASY LIVING OF THE CONFERENCE-TOURING SCIENTIST.

YOU TAKE ONE WRONG CORNER IN A FOREIGN CITY, AND...HERE I AM.

AND WHERE'S HERE?

A REMOTE CAMP OF THE... WELL, WHAT DO WE CALL THEM?

INSURGENTS? GUNMEN? TERRORISTS? GUERRILLAS? IT IS ALL THE SAME.

THEY HAVE YINSEN, THE GREAT MEDICAL INNOVATOR, FOR COMBAT MEDICINE.

AND NOW THEY HAVE ANTHONY STARK, THE GREAT WEAPONEER.

YOU SEE THIS? THIS IS YOUR FUTURE NOW.

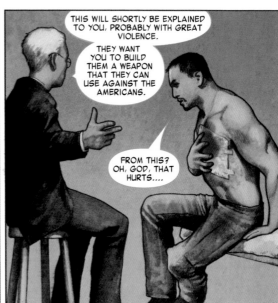

THIS WILL SHORTLY BE EXPLAINED TO YOU, PROBABLY WITH GREAT VIOLENCE.

THEY WANT YOU TO BUILD THEM A WEAPON THAT THEY CAN USE AGAINST THE AMERICANS.

FROM THIS? OH, GOD, THAT HURTS....

LUCKILY FOR YOU, YOUR WOUND IS FATAL. YOU WILL BE DEAD IN A WEEK.

THE SHRAPNEL IS MOVING. YOU WILL BE SLOWLY STABBED TO DEATH BY A CHUNK OF YOUR OWN MUNITION.

YINSEN IS NOT SO LUCKY, FOR HE IS TOUGHER THAN JOHN WAYNE'S OLD BOOTS AND WILL LIVE FOREVER.

I CAN'T GIVE THESE PEOPLE A WEAPON.

IF YOU TRY HARD, YOU COULD PERHAPS MAKE YOURSELF DIE FIRST.

YOU'RE NOT HELPING, YINSEN.

YOU ARE LUCKY TO HAVE ME AS YOUR FRIEND, WHITEY.

...YES, I AM.

AT THE CONFERENCE... YOU WERE TALKING ABOUT HELPING LAND MINE VICTIMS IN KOREA.

MAGNETIC WOUND EXCISION.

I CANNOT REMOVE THE SHRAPNEL. IT PRESSES ON YOUR HEART. THERE COULD BE A RUPTURE.

NOT REMOVE IT-- HOLD IT.

HOLD IT IN PLACE, STOP IT WORKING ITSELF DEEPER.

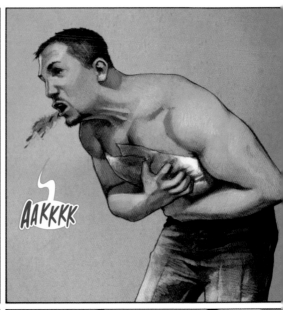

AAKKKK

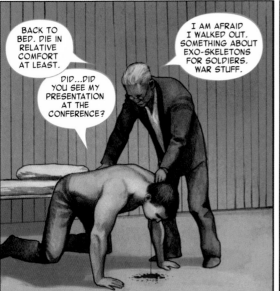

BACK TO BED. DIE IN RELATIVE COMFORT AT LEAST.

I AM AFRAID I WALKED OUT. SOMETHING ABOUT EXO-SKELETONS FOR SOLDIERS. WAR STUFF.

DID...DID YOU SEE MY PRESENTATION AT THE CONFERENCE?

IT WASN'T FOR WAR. THAT WAS JUST TO GET THE FUNDING.

YOU CAN'T JUST...WISH THE FUTURE INTO BEING. IT HAS TO BE PAID FOR.

EVEN THE MUNITIONS... WERE JUST STEALING MONEY FROM THE ARMY FOR THE REAL WORK.

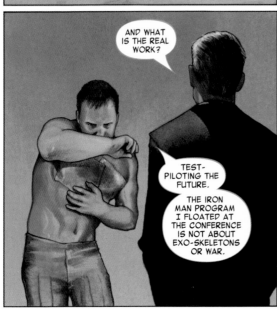

AND WHAT IS THE REAL WORK?

TEST-PILOTING THE FUTURE.

THE IRON MAN PROGRAM I FLOATED AT THE CONFERENCE IS NOT ABOUT EXO-SKELETONS OR WAR.

IT'S ABOUT BECOMING BETTER.

IT'S ABOUT BRINGING ON THE FUTURE.

THE EARLIEST STAGES OF ADAPTING MACHINE TO MAN AND MAKING US GREAT.

WE'RE GOING TO MAKE A PROTOTYPE IRON MAN OUT OF THIS.

A WEARABLE WEAPON FOR OUR HOSTS.

AND YOU'RE GOING TO BUILD A MAGNETIC FIELD GENERATOR INTO THE CHEST PLATE.

WE'RE GOING TO BUILD SOMETHING THAT KEEPS ME ALIVE LONG ENOUGH TO GET US BOTH OUT OF HERE.

BECAUSE MY WORK ISN'T FINISHED YET.

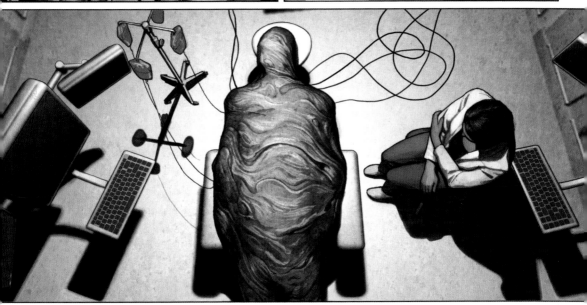

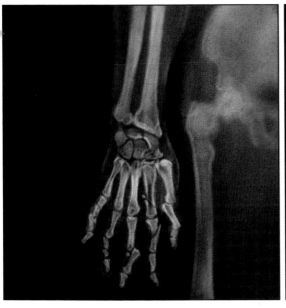

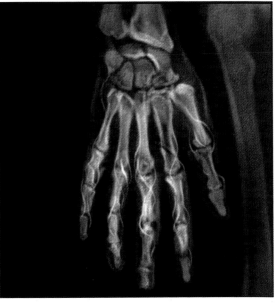

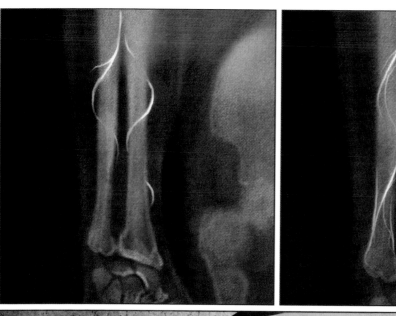

I TELL YOU...EITHER IT'S FINISHED, OR I AM.

IT IS DONE. AND PROBABLY SO ARE YOU.

QUICKLY, NOW.

UUHHHH

TONY?
TONY, ARE
YOU WELL?

TONY, CAN
YOU HEAR
ME?

TONY, CAN
YOU HEAR
ME?

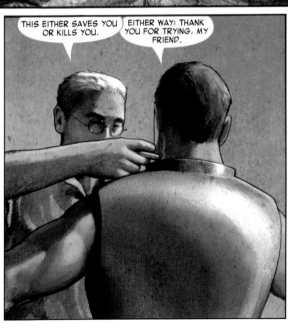

THIS EITHER SAVES YOU
OR KILLS YOU.

EITHER WAY: THANK
YOU FOR TRYING, MY
FRIEND.

DAMN YOU
FOR TRYING
THIS, TONY.

THIS ISN'T
HOW IT WAS
SUPPOSED
TO BE.

BEEN A HELL OF A WEEK... HASN'T IT?

THE NEXT BIT'S GOING TO BE REALLY INTERESTING.

SAY HELLO TO THE IRON MAN, YOU TERRORIST SCUM.

YOU PEOPLE WANTED STARK MICROMUNITIONS?

HAVE SOME.

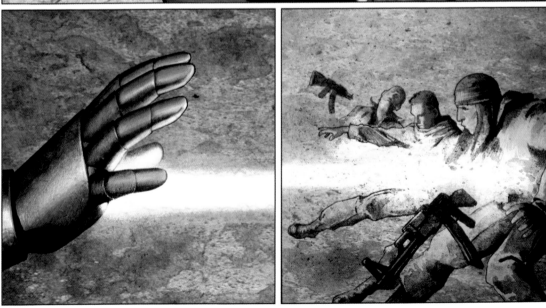

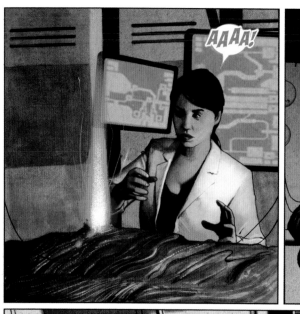
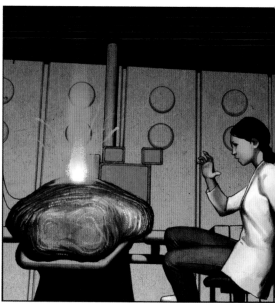
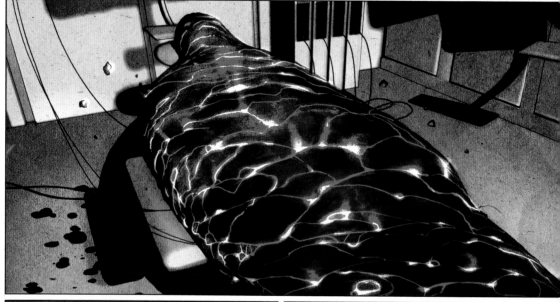
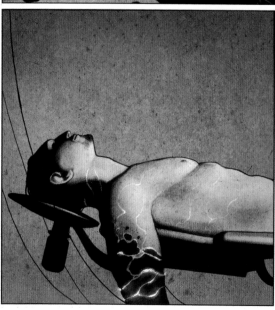
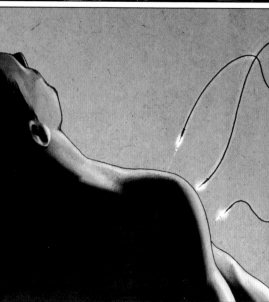

I'M ALIVE.

I'LL BE DAMNED.

TONY? DON'T TRY TO MOVE.

I AM SO SICK OF PEOPLE SAYING THAT TO ME.

HOW LONG WAS I OUT?

24 HOURS. THIS IS WAY TOO FAST.

I MADE A FEW ALTERATIONS TO YOUR PROGRAM WHILE YOU WERE OUT OF THE ROOM. REMOVED SOME SAFETIES.

YOU DID WHAT? TURN IT DOWN. I THINK I'VE GROWN NEW EAR TISSUE.

LET'S SEE IF THE OTHER STUFF I GREW WORKS.

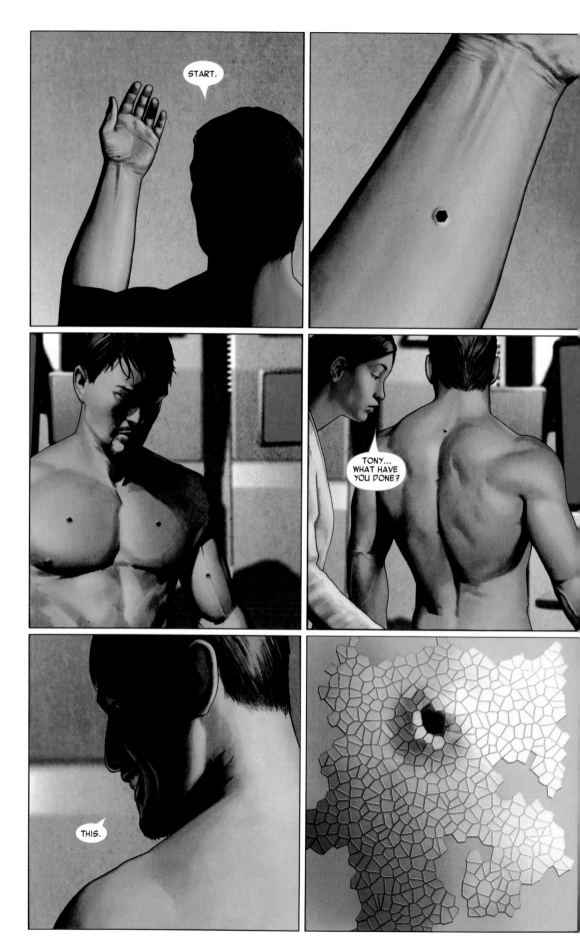

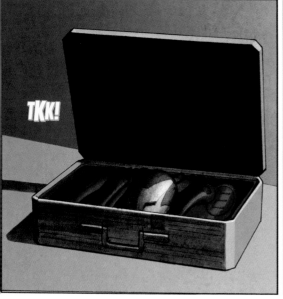

...MY GOD.

IRON MAN, INSIDE AND OUT.

WE HAVE TO RUN SOME TESTS. THE STRAIN ON YOUR INTERNAL ORGANS...

GREW NEW ONES.

I NEED TO GO TO WORK NOW. MALLEN'S STILL OUT THERE, AND HE'S A DAY CLOSER TO WASHINGTON, D.C.

WE DON'T KNOW WHERE HE IS.

I DO.

MAYA, I CAN SEE THROUGH SATELLITES NOW.

Iron Man

Written by Warren Ellis
Illustrated by Adi Granov

Washington, DC

"Extremis"

Lettering by UC's Randy Genti
Assistant Editors: Schmidt, Laeer, and Sitters
Editor: Tom Brevoor

Six of Six

Editor in Chief: Joe Quesac
Publisher: Dan Buckle

EVACUATION
OF THE AREA IS
COMPLETE, IRON
MAN. HE'S ALL
YOURS.

THANK
YOU.

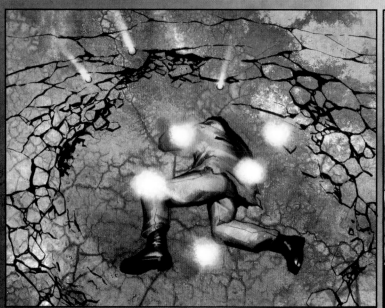

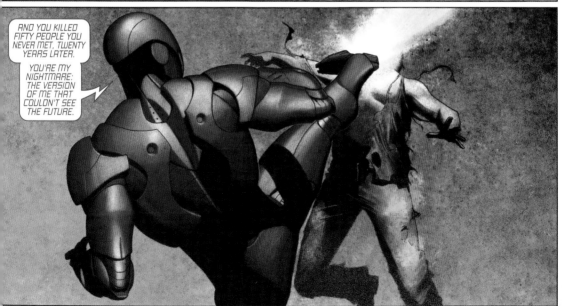

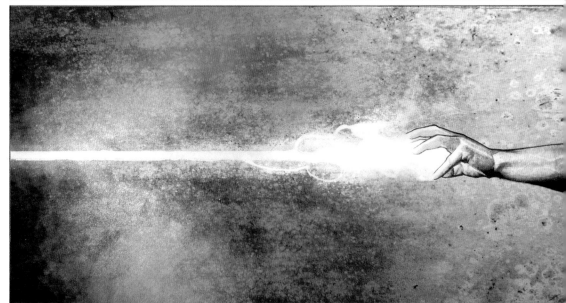

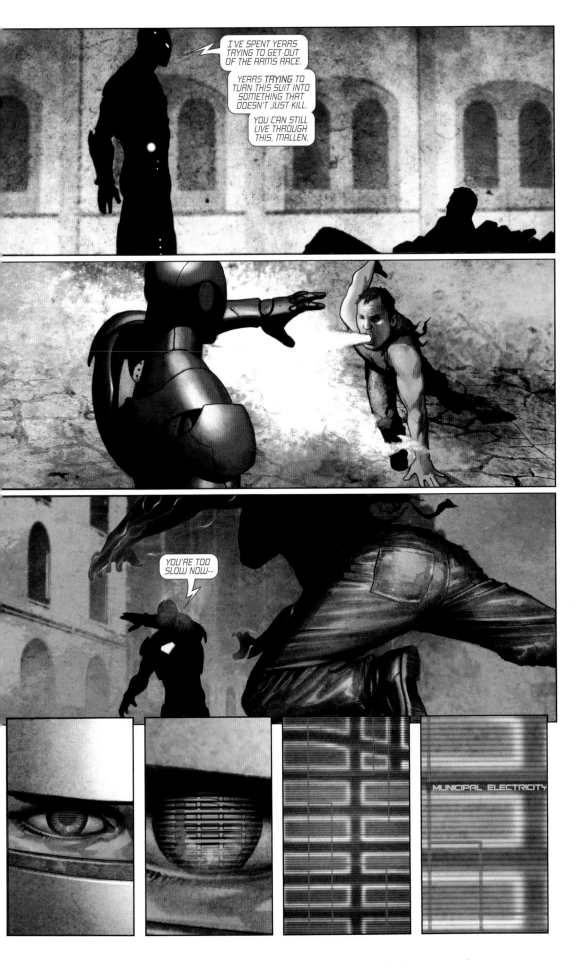

OH
GODDD...

I ONLY LEFT YOU ALIVE IN TEXAS BECAUSE I WAS BUSY--

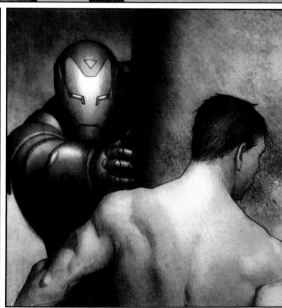

HA!

DID IT AGAIN--

KLANG!

RRRRAAAAH!!

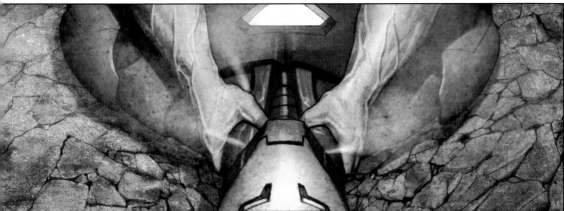

MALLEN... FOR GOD'S SAKE... DON'T MAKE ME...

THERE ISN'T ANY FUTURE!

I'M GOING TO KILL IT!

AAHKK!

UK
HRRR

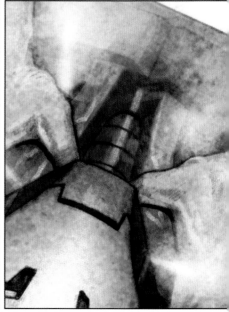

GKK
MALLEN
YOU
STUPID--

FUMP!

DAMN
YOU.

DAMN YOU
FOR MAKING
ME DO THAT.

ONE THING
LEFT TO DO.

THE WORST
THING.

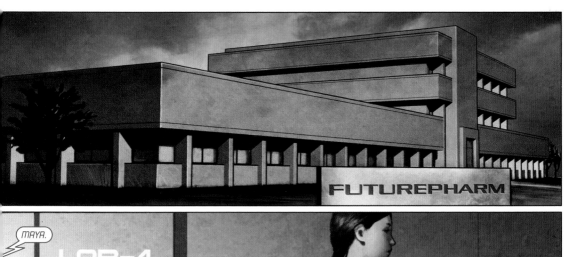

FUTUREPHARM

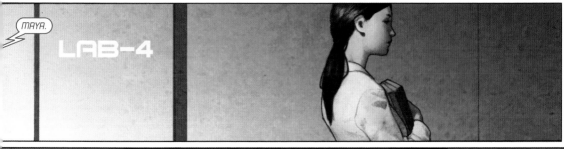

MAYA.

LAB-4

IT TAKES TWO KEYS TO OPEN THE EXTREMIS VAULT.

YOUR BOSS HAD ONE. YOU HAD ONE.

HE COULDN'T GET INTO THE VAULT TO STEAL THE EXTREMIS DOSE ON HIS OWN.

MP

I'VE HAD TIME TO DO SOME THINKING.

AND MY NEW SUIT WIRES ME INTO ALL KINDS OF NETWORKS.

I KNOW, MAYA.

ARTIST'S GALLERY
Iron Man

Over the years, Iron Man's armour has been redesigned by numerous creators. Some are mere refinements of the classic design, whilst others are more complex mission specific variations. Below are some of the most memorable Iron Man makeovers.

GREY ARMOUR

Designed by Jack Kirby and Don Heck. From **Tales of Suspense #39** (1963)

GOLD FINISH

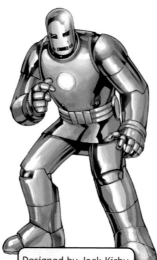

Designed by Jack Kirby and Don Heck. From **Tales of Suspense #40** (1963)

RED AND GOLD ARMOUR

Designed by Steve Ditko. From **Tales of Suspense #48** (1963)

Mk 2 RED AND GOLD ARMOUR

Designed by Gene Colan. From **Tales of Suspense #85** (1967)

SPACE ARMOUR

Designed by John Romita Jr. From **Iron Man #142** (1981)

STEALTH ARMOUR

Designed by John Romita Jr. From **Iron Man** #152 (1981)

SILVER CENTURION ARMOUR

Designed by Mark Bright. From **Iron Man** #200 (1985)

DEEP SEA ARMOUR

Designed by Mark Bright. From **Iron Man** #218 (1987)

WAR MACHINE ARMOUR

Designed by Kev Hopgood. From **Iron Man** #281 (1992)

THORBUSTER ARMOUR

Designed by Alan Davis. From **Iron Man** Vol 3 #64 (2003)

HULKBUSTER ARMOUR

Designed by John Romita Jr. From **World War Hulk** #1 (2007)

THE WRITER

Warren Ellis

REX FEATURES

FUTUREPROOF

A MAVERICK writer who began his career on the fringes of Britain's comics industry, **Warren Ellis's** earliest published work was as a contributor to *Flying Pig's Food for Thought*. This 1985 one-shot, published to raise funds for the Ethiopian famine relief, also featured work by other comic book heavy hitters such as **Grant Morrison** and **Alan Moore.** Five years later he made his professional debut with a six-pager in *Deadline #24.* Further UK stories followed with his first ongoing character, **Lazarus Churchyard,** appearing in all seven issues of *Blast!.* Described by some as cyberpunk (although the writer prefers "Decadent Science Fiction"), it was this 1991 series that brought him to the attention of US publishers.

In 1994 Ellis took over Marvel's *Hellstorm: Prince of Lies.* He only wrote 10 issues before the title was axed but his idiosyncratic reworking of the House of Ideas' Son of Satan began to draw attention from the comic-reading cognoscenti. As his star rose, more work followed including *Thor, Wolverine* and *Excalibur* - a British-based spin-off from Marvel's mighty X-Men franchise.

While continuing to write for Marvel he began working for DC's **WildStorm** imprint. There he took over *StormWatch* before launching a 1999 spin-off with artist **Bryan Hitch.** Considered a sea change in the way superhero team titles were written, *The Authority* was a cinematic super-action series for which Ellis coined the term "widescreen comics". Two years earlier, the Southend-on-Sea resident had been one of the innovative writers who helped launch DC's **Helix** line, a new imprint that specialized in sci-fi stories. His contribution was the **Darick Robertson**-illustrated *Transmetropolitan.* Later transferred to the Vertigo imprint, this long-running series offered Ellis a forum from which to indulge his penchant for socio-cultural commentary, embracing such trans-humanist themes as nanotechnology, cryonics, mind transfer, and human enhancement.

Wholeheartedly embracing new technology, Warren Ellis has a massive online presence and following. You can find more news on his up-coming projects and his thoughts on science, politics and life in general at www.warrenellis.com.

SAME SUIT, NEW WAR...

Given the task of bringing Ol' Shellhead's origins up to date, Ellis detached Tony Stark from his original background in Vietnam, exchanging it for modern day Afghanistan. Keeping the Marvel Universe in general at arm's length provided him with the freedom to rework the Golden Avenger without having to consider outside and/or historical influences. As the writer revealed, "I re-read only the very earliest issues, as I recall. These things only work when you scrape off the barnacles of accrued continuity and expose the face of the thing that made people interested in the character in the first place."

IN EXTREMIS

It was his capacity for innovation and his refusal to be burdened by the trappings of the past that made him an ideal candidate to relaunch **Iron Man**, especially when coupled with his deep and abiding interest in cutting edge technology.

The writer's work on the series came about after then Marvel editor-in-chief **Joe Quesada** told him that he was unable to get a useful handle on the character. "I commented that he was the test pilot for the future. I'm pretty sure everything came from that. He emerged from a time when you could still get away with an armaments manufacturer as hero. When you look at the character's life in print since then, you can draw a line through it all and find a man who's trying to get away from what he was and devoting everything he's got to bringing on outbreaks of the future."

Those thoughts were the genesis of the Adi Granov-illustrated *Extremis*. Running through the first six issues of 2004's Iron Man relaunch, the highly significant serial has provided the underpinning of all the Iron Man stories that have followed. More than that, it was also a major influence on Iron Man's big screen incarnation.

Ellis's credits are numerous and range from the outer reaches of experimentation to the very centre of the comic's mainstream superhero market. Unconfined by genres and traditions, whatever he writes is groundbreaking and he continues to pioneer new concepts and ways of reworking existing properties.

THE ARTIST
Adi Granov

Fascinated by all things technical and scientific, Bosnian born artist **Adi Granov** is the perfect match for the armoured Avenger. Read on to discover his thoughts on drawing Iron Man.

IRON ARMOURER

First employed by Marvel in 2004, **Adi Granov** initially worked almost exclusively on cover artwork. His realistic, digitally painted style made him an instant hit with readers. Later that year, he was named by then Editor-In-Chief **Joe Quesada** as one of Marvels 'Young Guns', cementing his position as a Marvel fan-favourite.

Prior to his time at Marvel, Adi had worked for both **Devil's Due** and **Dreamwave**, working on numerous projects including *G.I. Joe* and interior pages for a series called *Necro-War*. Though he enjoyed cover work, Adi always intended to return to interior work, but was waiting for the right project to come along. When Editor **Tom Brevoort** offered him the opportunity to work with **Warren Ellis** on a new Iron Man story, he knew it was a perfect match and eagerly accepted.

Extremis was an instant hit, but it wasn't just comic fans who were thrilled with his work. Iron Man movie Director **Jon Favreau** was so impressed that he bought Adi on board to help with concept designs for the movie. He also continued to provide concept work for *Iron Man 2* and is currently working on a new suit design for the up-coming *Avengers* movie.

How did you break into drawing comics and was it something you'd always wanted to do?

Adi Granov: I was an illustrator and designer for many years before getting work in comics, and I always saw comic books as just another outlet for my work. I was a huge fan of European comics, as that's what was available where I grew up, so it definitely has always been a passion of mine.

Who would you say are the main influences on your comic book work?

AG: Mostly European artists such as Moebius, Bilal and Liberatore, as well as American poster artists Drew Struzan and Amsel. There are many similarities between the works of all of these guys, and a lot of their influence can be seen in my artwork. I didn't start reading American comics until I was already into my 20s, so although I've been inspired and influenced by them since, they didn't form a foundation to what I do.

What was it like to work on Iron Man? Were you a fan of the character before?

AG: Aside from the look of the character, I knew next to nothing about Iron Man. It was probably a good thing, as Warren Ellis and I were tasked with re-booting him, so it was perfect that I could approach him with fresh eyes.

How was it working with Warren Ellis on Extremis. Was he the kind of writer that wants to see every page on the fly? Or did he leave you to it?

AG: He's mostly hands off,

which I like, and left me to do what I do. I love working with Warren and consider him one of the best writers in the industry.

What was your favourite part of the story to draw?

AG: It's been a long time since I worked on it... Probably the action scenes with Mallen. He was an unhinged, violent character and it was fun to draw the craziness involving him.

Do you have a favourite hero or villain to draw?

AG: Hard to say, as I try to make anything I work on to my liking and make the best of it. I really enjoy drawing the extreme characters like the Hulk, but on the other hand another of my favourites is the Black Widow. I always found Captain America challenging, so that's one of the reasons I am working on a Cap book at the moment, to try to put my stamp on it.

You have a specific technique to your work using watercolours/gouache and photoshop, how long did it take to complete Extremis, from start to finish with this method?

AG: My technique is mostly pencil based with watercolour, gouache, etc. playing a supporting role to add depth, and then finally coloured with Photoshop. My wife Tamsin often helps with colour separations/flats, and I do the rendering. It took a long time to do the six issues and covers. Around a year and a half...

How long does it take you to produce a single page of comic artwork?

AG: It largely depends on the contents of the page and the number of panels, but roughly between a day and a half and three days.

How did it feel to do concept work for the Iron Man movies?

AG: It was exciting because it was working to a very large audience, but as far as the work itself goes it was fairly normal, lots of drawing just like all my other work. In many ways movie work is less challenging than comic work.

Finally, Iron Man's armour has been constantly redesigned by different artists. Do you have a particular favourite?

AG: As bad as it may sound, I have to say my favourite are the Mark 2 and 3 movie armour. Phil Saunders and I took a lot of time to design it and make it right, and then the Stan Winston guys built it, which really made it very special and the most remarkable piece of work I've ever been involved with. It was even exhibited at the Metropolitan Museum in NY!

FURTHER READING

If you've enjoyed the style and art in this graphic novel, you may be interested in exploring some of these books too.

Marvel Platinum: The Definitive Iron Man

At the book shop:
ISBN: 9781905239856

Ultimate Comics: Armour Wars

At the book shop:
ISBN: 9781846534416

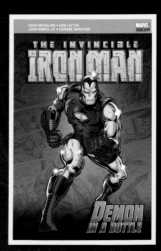

Iron Man: Demon In A Bottle
Volume 1 of the Ultimate Marvel Graphic Novels Collection

At the book shop:
ISBN: 9781846531293

Astonishing X-Men: Ghost Box

At the book shop:
ISBN: 9780785127888

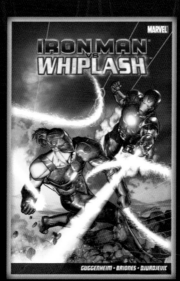

Iron Man Versus Whiplash

At the book shop:
ISBN: 9781846534508

Thunderbolts: Faith In Monsters
Volume 56 of the Ultimate Marvel Graphic Novels Collection

At the book shop:
ISBN: 9780785125662